Editor in Chief:
Sharon Coan, M.S. Ed.

Art Director:
Elayne Roberts

Cover Series Designer:
Tina Macabitas

Art Coordinator:
Cheri Macoubrie Wilson

Product Manager:
Phil Garcia

Imaging:
Alfred Lau

Publishers:
Rachelle Cracchiolo, M.S. Ed.
Mary Dupuy Smith, M.S. Ed.

INTERNET ACTIVITIES FOR MATH

PRIMARY

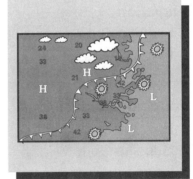

Author:

Alain Chirinian

Teacher Created Materials, Inc.
6421 Industry Way
Westminster, CA   92683
www.teachercreated.com
ISBN-1-57690-191-2

TABLE OF CONTENTS

TABLE OF CONTENTS *(cont.)*

INTRODUCTION

This book is designed to take full advantage of the most important new learning opportunity ever available to our students: the Internet. In order to be competitive thinkers, workers, and productive citizens with high self-esteem, the young people we teach must become familiar with this latest communication tool. *Internet Activities for Math* presents a special way for students to launch themselves onto the World Wide Web, visiting virtual zoos, universities, museums, and even outer space while learning essential math skills—and having fun while doing it!

Most of the pages are self-contained activities, although in some instances several pages are used as a more long-term, involved activity. This should be taken into account when planning your Internet access time at school. Teacher pages are provided for each activity or group of similar activities to help familiarize you with what objectives are to be accomplished, as well as including information linking the activity to the NCTM standards. These standards can be accessed on the Internet at http://www.enc.org/reform/index.htm. In addition, enrichment opportunities are suggested in most instances.

Internet Activities for Math assumes that you have a basic knowledge of Internet use and terminology and can move freely around the Web as needed. It is important that you upgrade your browser to the latest version available and enable its Java capabilities. Furthermore, you should take advantage of the many helper applications, or "plug-ins," available, such as *Shockwave* and *Real Audio,* for best results on some Web sites.

It is highly recommended that you visit each Web site in advance of assigning any activity. This will ensure that the Web sites you want to visit are still active. With the fast pace of change on the Internet, some sites may have moved or "gone dark" in the interim since this book was written. Previewing the sites also provides you with the opportunity to bookmark the sites ahead of time so that students do not spend a great deal of time entering and re-entering the URLs.

One method of cheating the fickle nature of the Web is to use a Web "whacking" program, such as Web Buddy, produced by DataViz. Web Buddy will allow you to "whack" or download a single Web page or even an entire Web site, including the links and graphics. It stores the Web pages on your hard drive where they can be accessed with your browser at a later date—even if the page or site has disappeared! Students can enjoy the Web-based activities without the associated wait times during peak Internet hours, or the dreaded "Not Found" error. Teacher Created Materials publishes Web Buddy, a book filled with classroom projects and tips on using the Web Buddy software which is included on a CD-ROM. It is available for $39.95 by calling (800) 662-4321.

Teacher Created Materials is dedicated to providing teachers with updated links to sites which have become inactive. You can visit our Web site to find these updates or to provide feedback about this or any of our publications.

http://www.teachercreated.com/updates.html

NEWSY NUMBERS

Objective(s):

Students will...

- locate and identify descriptive numbers in a newspaper.

Materials Needed:

- computer
- student activity sheet

Web Site(s):

- http://www.latimes.com
- http://www.ocregister.com

Teaching the Lesson:

Students will be exposed to a variety of numerical data in this activity, including statistics, percentages, and fractions. You may need to explain this to them individually or keep a log of questions and discuss them as a class afterwards. Explain the uses of percentages to express sale prices, fractions in demographics, and the like. Any of the numbers and statistics provide excellent lesson integration opportunities, especially since students will choose different pages to look at in the newspaper.

NCTM Standards: 1, 2, 3, 4, 6, 9, 10, 11, 12, 13

NEWSY NUMBERS

Name: _____

Date: _____

Go to:

http://www.latimes.com

or

http://www.ocregister.com

Numbers are used every day in the newspapers, magazines and many other places to describe things. Give examples of numbers you find that describe...

1. the price of something.

   What is it? _____
   How much does it cost? _____

2. sports scores.

Team	**Score**
_____	_____
_____	_____
_____	_____

3. a statistic.

   _____

4. a percent (hint: look at the weather forecast).

   _____

5. a distance or length measurement.

   _____

ODD AND EVEN

Objective(s):

Students will...

- explore and identify odd and even numbers.

Materials Needed:

- computer
- student activity sheet

Web Site(s):

- http://theoak.com/gary/index.html
- http://www.ratshole.com/burgcycl.html

Teaching the Lesson:

This lesson uses pictures of furniture and of a trike to practice using odd and even numbers and to derive a general rule for adding the numbers together. Students may need help to come up with a general rule that can be tested.

NCTM Standards: 1, 2, 3, 4, 6, 9, 13

ODD AND EVEN

Name: _____

Date: _____

Go to:

http://theoak.com/gary/index.html

Click on a link to find a chair.

1. How many legs does each chair have?

   _____

Click on a link to find a table.

2. How many legs does the table have?

   _____

3. How many legs are on four chairs? Is this an odd or even number?

   _____

   _____

4. How many are all the legs for the four chairs and the table?

   _____

5. What happens when you add even numbers together?

   _____

   _____

   _____

ODD AND EVEN *(cont.)*

Name: _____

Date: _____

Go to:

http://www.ratshole.com/burgcycl.html

Here you will find an interesting kind of motorcycle—a trike!

6. Is there an odd or even number of wheels on a trike?

_____

7. How many wheels are there when you add together the wheels on two trikes? Is this odd or even?

_____

8. Think about the question above. Can you decide on a rule about adding togther odd numbers? Wait, not so fast! Now add together the number of wheels on THREE trikes! Odd or even?

_____

9. What happens every time you add TWO odd numbers together?

_____

_____

_____

10. What happens every time you add THREE ODD numbers together?

_____

_____

_____

FIND THE NUMBERS

Objective(s):

Students will...

- locate and identify numbers on an image.

Materials Needed:

- computer
- student activity sheet

Web Site(s):

- http://www.ctw.org/preschool/games/character/0,1170,2031,00.html

Teaching the Lesson:

Students who have difficulty with shapes will find this activity rewarding because they can find familiar numbers to search for instead.

NCTM Standards: 6, 9, 13

FIND THE NUMBERS

Name: _____

Date: _____

Go to:

http://www.ctw.org/preschool/games/character/0,1170,2031,00.html

Click on the picture where you find each number.

Where did you find the number...

one? _____

two? _____

three? _____

four? _____

five? _____

six? _____

seven? _____

eight? _____

nine? _____

MONSTROUS MATH

Objective(s):

Students will...

- count various parts of a "monster."
- compute using addition and subtraction.

Materials Needed:

- computer
- student activity sheet

Web Site(s):

- http://www.lifelong.com/lifelong_universe/AcademicWorld/MonsterMath/NTEng/NTHowToPlay.html

Teaching the Lesson:

This lesson puts together students' pattern recognition and computation skills. They keep a running record of their progress through the game. The game provides feedback to their answers immediately. This lesson can be supplemented by any competitive math game.

NCTM Standards: 1, 2, 3, 4, 6, 7, 8, 9, 13

MONSTROUS MATH

Name: _____

Date: _____

Go to:

http://www.lifelong.com/lifelong_universe/AcademicWorld/MonsterMath/NT Eng/NTHowToPlay.html

Follow the directions on the screen to help you make a monster!

Write down your answer to each question on this page.

Then click on your choice to see if it was right!

If you get the answer right, you get to go to the next page!

1. Your answer to question one: _____

2. Your answer to question two: _____

3. Your answer to question three: _____

4. Your answer to question four: _____

5. Your answer to question five: _____

6. Your answer to question six: _____

7. Your answer to question seven: _____

8. Your answer to question eight: _____

9. Your answer to question nine: _____

10. Your answer to question ten: _____

How did you do? How many questions did you get right the first time?

_____

_____

_____

HOLIDAY COUNTERS

Objective(s):

Students will...

- use counting skills to determine the number of various creatures on each Web page.

Materials Needed:

- computer
- student activity sheet

Web Site(s):

- http://www.xmission.com/~emailbox/halloween.htm
- http://www.xmission.com/~emailbox/halloween2.htm

Teaching the Lesson:

These lessons are ideal for fall holiday seasons, and an introduction to or a review of counting skills. Make sure students wait for all the images to load on the page before starting to count, or they will miss something!

NCTM Standards: 1, 2, 3, 6, 13

HOLIDAY COUNTERS

Name: _____

Date: _____

Go to:

http://www.xmission.com/~emailbox/halloween.htm

1. How many witches are on this page?

_____

2. How many jack-o'-lanterns are on this page?

_____

3. How many black cats are on this page?

_____

4. How many mummies are on this page?

_____

5. How many brooms are on this page?

_____

6. What holiday does this page remind you of?

_____

Student Activity Sheet

HOLIDAY COUNTERS *(cont.)*

Name: _____

Date: _____

Go to:

http://www.xmission.com/~emailbox/halloween2.htm

1. How many bats can you find on this page?

   _____

2. How many flying witches can you see?

   _____

3. How many cats are wearing hats?

   _____

4. How many cats have a shadow?

   _____

5. How many moons are there on this page?

   _____

6. Write down how many jack-o'-lanterns are on this page.

   _____

HOLIDAY COUNTERS *(cont.)*

Name: _____

Date: _____

Go to:

http://www.xmission.com/~emailbox/christmas.htm

1. How many kittens on this page are trying to keep warm by the fireplace?

   _____

2. Write down how many kittens are outside in the snow.

   _____

3. How many cats on this page are sitting near a Christmas tree?

   _____

4. How many cats are wearing hats?

   _____

5. How many cats are wearing bows?

   _____

COUNT BY NUMBERS

Objective(s):

Students will...

- count by ones, twos and threes, using animal characteristics.

Materials Needed:

- computer
- student activity sheet

Web Site(s):

- http://www.sirius.com/~fonzilla/lcants.jpg
- http://www.seaworld.org/animal_bytes/walrusab.html
- http://www.til.org/~whales/narwhal.html

Teaching the Lesson:

Counting lessons can be done orally before or after these activities. Show students that they can "do math" in their heads by counting this way. As with any of these activities, "link" this topic to those on the various Web pages, including the purpose of tusks and insect behavior.

NCTM Standards: 1, 2, 3, 4, 6, 8, 9, 10, 13

COUNT BY NUMBERS

Name: _____

Date: _____

Go to:

http://www.sirius.com/~fonzilla/lcants.jpg

1. How many ants are in this picture?

   _____

2. How many would there be if each ant brought another ant with her?

   _____

Suppose you are watching an ant trail. You see that every second, two ants walk by you.

3. How many ants would pass you in two seconds?

   _____

4. How many ants would pass you in five seconds?

   _____

5. How many ants would pass you in twenty seconds?

   _____

That's a lot of ants!

COUNT BY NUMBERS *(cont.)*

Name: _____

Date: _____

Go to:

http://www.seaworld.org/animal_bytes/walrusab.html

1. Count the number of tusks on the walrus. How many do you see?

   _____

2. If there were two walruses, how many tusks would you see?

   _____

3. Imagine four walruses lying in a row on the beach. How many tusks would there be all together?

   _____

4. How much of the walrus' life is spent in the water?

   _____

5. Would you say that this is some, most, or all of their life?

   _____

Go to:

http://www.til.org/~whales/narwhal.html

6. How many tusks are on the narwhal compared to the walrus?

   _____

7. How many tusks would three narwhals have all together?

   _____

8. If three narwhals met three walruses, how many tusks would there be all together?

   _____

HOT HATCH MARKS

Objective(s):

Students will...

- identify whales and dolphins.
- record sightings.
- count by fives.

Materials Needed:

- computer
- student activity sheet

Web Site(s):

- http://www.premier1.net/~iamdavid/children.html

Teaching the Lesson:

Students will need to search carefully to find the instances where whales and dolphins are mentioned on this Web site. They will be tempted to click on some of these links, so monitor their progress carefully. Discuss the idea of hatch marks and how they can be used as an alternate number system.

NCTM Standards: 1, 2, 3, 4, 6, 7, 9, 13

HOT HATCH MARKS

Name: _____

Date: _____

You are going to search a Web site for whales and dolphins. Each time you see a picture of a dolphin or whale or see the words dolphin or whale on the Web page, you need to make a hatch mark in the box below. After four hatch marks, make a slanted one across the other four as your fifth one, like this

$$\cancel{||||}$$

This counts as five. Then start the next set of marks in the box below it.

Go to:

http://www.premier1.net/~iamdavid/children.html

This page takes a little while to load, so be patient.

Whale and Dolphin Words and Pictures

Total Hatch Marks: _____

DON'T GET SHORTCHANGED

Objective(s):

Students will...

- compute appropriate change, using addition and/or subtraction.

Materials Needed:

- computer
- student activity sheet

Web Site(s):

- http://www.etoys.com/

Teaching the Lesson:

Students simulate making change in a store in this activity. It is one of the many activities you should use to help students apply their money skills along with the addition and subtraction they have already learned or are in the process of learning.

NCTM Standards: 1, 2, 3, 4, 6, 7, 8, 12, 13

DON'T GET SHORTCHANGED

Name: _____

Date: _____

Pretend that you work at a toy store. It is very important that you make the correct change for each and every customer.

Go to

http://www.etoys.com/

Your first customer has bought just one item, a touch and crawl baby doll. This item costs $21.99. The customer hands you 22 dollars. How much change does he get?

Change:

You must recommend two toys for your next customer. She wants to buy a toy for her niece and another for her nephew. She has 40 dollars. Your job is to find two toys and decide how much change you will give her after you add up the costs of the toys. Remember not to spend more than forty dollars!

Name of toy: **Cost:**

_____   _____

_____   _____

Total Cost:

_____

Change due to customer:

_____

CATS, CATS, CATS

Objective(s):

Students will...

- use addition and subtraction skills to count cats.

Materials Needed:

- computer
- student activity sheet

Web Site(s):

- http://www.xmission.com/~emailbox/icons.htm

Teaching the Lesson:

Students should have some concept of addition and subtraction by the time they finish these activities. They can serve as primers for more advanced topics or just practice for students who already have mastered them.

NCTM Standards: 1, 2, 3, 4, 6, 7, 8, 13

CATS, CATS, CATS

Name: _____

Date: _____

Go to:

http://www.xmission.com/~emailbox/icons.htm

Directions: Find the cats. Count all the cats.

How many cats are left when...

1. one cat runs away?

    _____

2. one cat is adopted?

    _____

3. two cats go to live with a neighbor?

    _____

4. four cats disappear and decide to live with a witch?

    _____

CATS, CATS, CATS (cont.)

Name: _____

Date: _____

Go to:

http://www.xmission.com/~emailbox/icons.htm

Directions: Look carefully at the cats on this Web page. Answer the questions below.

1. How many cats are in the first row?

   _____

2. How many black cats are in the second row?

   _____

3. How many cats with green eyes are in the third row?

   _____

4. How many cats have their own home page in row four?

   _____

5. How many "cartoon" cats are in row five?

   _____

YEARS GONE BY

Objective(s):

Students will...

- find historical data from the recent and more distant past.
- use addition and subtraction to compare historical events.

Materials Needed:

- computer
- student activity sheet

Web Site(s):

- http://w3.mlr.com/mlr/ahc/chrono/c2.html
- http://www.srh.noaa.gov/FTPROOT/LCH/txhur.htm
- http://www.nhc.noaa.gov

Teaching the Lesson:

These lessons can be integrated with U.S. history topics, as well as science. Creating a time line would be a valuable extension to this activity. Students would also appreciate learning more about other natural disasters in addition to hurricanes.

NCTM Standards: 2, 3, 4, 6, 7, 8, 13

YEARS GONE BY

Name: _____

Date: _____

Go to:

http://w3.mlr.com/mlr/ahc/chrono/c2.html

After the Civil War in our country, many important things happened that changed the United States forever. In this activity, use your math skills to figure out the number of years between these events in history.

1. In what year did the Civil War begin?

   _____

2. How many years after the Civil War began was Abraham Lincoln assasinated?

   _____

3. When was the electric light invented?

   _____

4. How many years after the electric light was invented did the Spanish-American War begin?

   _____

5. In what year was President McKinley assassinated?

   _____

YEARS GONE BY *(cont.)*

Name: _____

Date: _____

Go to:

http://www.srh.noaa.gov/FTPROOT/LCH/txhur.htm

Hurricanes are one of the most powerful forces in nature. They often cause great damage and even loss of life. This Web page shows you the dates of some of the most deadly hurricanes in history.

1. In what year did Ben Franklin begin to study the movement of hurricanes?

   _____

2. How many years after that did the deadliest storm on record happen?

   _____

3. The "Racer's Storm" wrecked three ships off of North Carolina in what year?

   _____

4. How many years after the Racer's Storm did a hurricane kill 700 people in Georgia and South Carolina?

   _____

FIGURING OUT FISH

Objective(s):

Students will...

- estimate the number of fish in a fishbowl.

Materials Needed:

- student activity sheet
- computer

Web Site(s):

- http://www.cling.gu.se/~cl2lryd/allfish.html#various

Teaching the Lesson:

This activity should be done in conjunction with your lessons on estimation. You may need to help the students in their research regarding aquarium capacity, or you can do it as a class. Having an aquarium handy for students to observe would enable them to do the bonus.

NCTM Standards: 4, 5, 9

FIGURING OUT FISH

Name: _____

Date: _____

There are ten goldfish in the picture below.

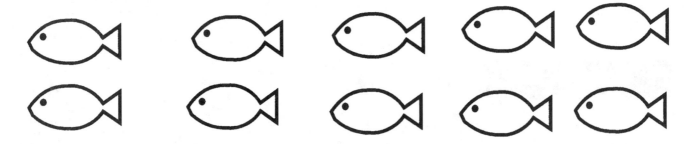

Without counting, can you estimate if there are more than or fewer than ten goldfish in each goldfish bowl below? Circle the bowl if it has more than ten, and leave it blank if there are fewer than ten.

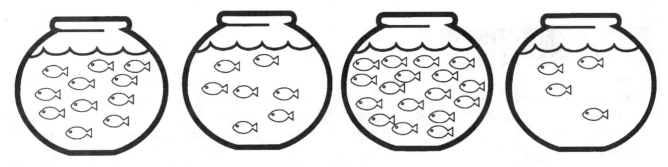

Go to:

http://www.cling.gu.se/~cl2lryd/allfish.html#various

Find out how to decide how many fish are enough for a fish tank.

Bonus: Check out a fish tank in your classroom or somewhere else in your school. Are the fish overcrowded? Explain why or why not.

_____

_____

I WORK FOR PEANUTS

Objective(s):

Students will...

- estimate and then revise their estimates to create a more accurate assessment of the number of peanuts in a jar.
- research peanut facts on the Internet.

Materials Needed:

- student activity sheet
- computer
- large jar of peanuts
- cups

Web Site(s):

- http://www.peanut-shellers.org/history.html
- http://www.azshops.com/Brittle/Nut-facts.html

Teaching the Lesson:

Use a large Mason jar or goldfish bowl for your peanuts. Use shelled nuts. Use this as an opportunity to discuss how one can estimate and revise estimates based on closer observation and research on a topic. Be sure you know how many peanuts are in the jar beforehand!

NCTM Standards: 1, 2, 3, 4, 5

I WORK FOR PEANUTS

Name: _____

Date: _____

Your teacher has a large jar full of peanuts. Everyone will have a chance to look carefully at the jar. After you have taken your first look, write down your estimate of the number of peanuts in the jar.

First Estimate _____

Now your teacher will give you a peanut. Examine it carefully. Are you certain of your first estimate? You may write a new estimate for the number of peanuts in the jar if you wish.

Second Estimate_____

Go to:

http://www.peanut-shellers.org/history.html
http://www.azshops.com/Brittle/Nut-facts.html

Write down two facts you did not know about peanuts.

1. _____

2. _____

Your teacher will now give you a cup full of peanuts. Examine it carefully. Count the peanuts in the cup. Write this number down.

Peanuts in the Cup _____

You may now revise (change) your estimate of the number of peanuts in the jar one last time.

Third Estimate_____

Your teacher will now reveal the actual number of peanuts in the jar. Write down this number.

Actual Number of Peanuts _____

What is the difference between your last estimate and the actual number in the jar? Your first estimate?

_____

MINIVAN MANIA

Objective(s):

Students will...

- configure the seats in a minivan to accommodate different numbers of people and their equipment.

Materials Needed:

- computer
- student activity sheet

Web Site(s):

- http://www.plymouthcars.com/voyagers/frameset_voyagers.html

Teaching the Lesson:

Students must study the minivan carefully to see the possible seating arrangements. They may want to write down or draw the possibilities on a separate sheet of paper as they work through the combinations. This activity will hit home for many students because they may have a minivan in their family which is occasionally challenged for space.

NCTM Standards: 1, 2, 3, 4, 5, 6, 7, 8, 9, 13

MINIVAN MANIA

Name: _____

Date: _____

Go to:

http://www.plymouthcars.com/voyagers/frameset_voyagers.html

Suppose you were in charge of transportation for a championship soccer team. The team is going to play in the finals in a state across the country. You must make sure you have room for 11 players and two family members each, plus their luggage. There are seven minivans available to transport everyone.

Look at the picture of the minivan. You have a choice of seating for three, four, or six people.

What would be the best way to adjust the seating in the minivans and still have enough room for people and luggage?

_____

What would happen if one of the minivans broke down on the way? Would you be able to fit every person into the remaining minivans?

_____

If there were tickets for only the soccer players and one family member each, how many minivans would be needed to get to the championship?

_____

You have finally arrived at the stadium! Now everyone needs a place to stay overnight. Estimate how many motel rooms you would need if up to four people could stay in each room.

_____

_____

HOW ARE THEY SIMILAR?

Objective(s):

Students will...

- count and examine patterns in fish and insects.

Materials Needed:

- computer
- student activity sheet

Web Site(s):

- http://mgfx.com/Butterfly/Gallery/greg1.htm
- http://www.lam.mus.ca.us/lacmnh/departments/research/entomology/scarabs
- http://www.ku.ac.th/fish/mfish.html/fresh/afwindex.html

Teaching the Lesson:

This activity is another opportunity for students to recognize patterns in living things. Grouping things together, whether fish or kinds of coins, is an important skill. Since everything we see has a certain shape, emphasize that even though we sometimes can't describe a shape verbally (like a "fish" shape), we can tell how it is the same as and different from other shapes.

NCTM Standards: 2, 3, 4, 9, 13

HOW ARE THEY SIMILAR?

Name: _____ Date: _____

Go to:

http://mgfx.com/Butterfly/Gallery/greg1.htm

Click on at least three different butterfly pictures to make them larger.

1. Look carefully at one of the butterflies on the Web page. What are three things about it that make it a butterfly?

   _____

   _____

   _____

Go to:

http://www.lam.mus.ca.us/lacmnh/departments/research/entomology/scarabs/

Any of the pictures of beetles can be clicked to see them up close. Click on at least three different ones.

2. Look carefully at the beetles you see on this Web page. What are three things about it that make it a beetle?

   _____

   _____

   _____

3. Now see if you can think of two things that butterflies and beetles have in common.

   _____

   _____

4. Write down two things that make butterflies and beetles different.

   _____

   _____

HOW ARE THEY SIMILAR? *(cont.)*

Name: _____

Date: _____

Go to:

http://www.ku.ac.th/fish/mfish.html/fresh/afwindex.html

1. How many fish do you see in the bowl?

   _____

2. Can you find three things that all these fish have in common?

   _____

   _____

   _____

3. Click on one of the fish links on this page, and look at a different kind of fish from the ones you just saw. Write down two ways this fish is different and two ways that it is the same as the first group of fish you saw.

Different

_____

_____

Same

_____

_____

GUPPIES GONE WILD

Objective(s):

Students will...

- identify patterns and relationships in guppies.

Materials Needed:

- computer
- student activity sheet

Web Site(s):

- http://www.guppies.com/photos.shtml

Teaching the Lesson:

This lesson makes use of student abilities to recognize similarities and differences in shapes, colors, and other features of guppies. This is a good starting point to discuss why scientists group certain kinds of animals together (such as guppies) while separating them from others (a guppy is a fish but not the same kind of fish as a shark).

NCTM Standards: 1, 2, 3, 4, 9, 13

GUPPIES GONE WILD

Name: _____ Date: _____

Go to:

http://www.guppies.com/photos.shtml

Click on each guppy link that has the word sword in the name.

1. What do all the sword guppies have in common with each other?

_____

2. What are some of the differences you see in the sword guppies?

_____

Click on each guppy link that has the word mosaic in the name.

3. What do all the mosaic guppies have in common with each other?

_____

4. What are some of the differences you see in the mosaic guppies?

_____

5. Write down two ways the guppies you have seen are similar.

Same

_____

_____

6. Write down two ways the guppies you have seen are different.

Different

_____

FLOCK TOGETHER

Objective(s):

Students will...

- look up and define mathematical grouping words.

Materials Needed:

- computer
- student activity sheet

Web Site(s):

- http://www.infoseek.com/Facts?pg=deskref.html

Teaching the Lesson:

This simple lesson can help generate student interest in the animals mentioned that live in groups. A discussion of the advantages and disadvantages of solitary v. group life would be excellent here.

NCTM Standards: 2, 4, 6

FLOCK TOGETHER

Name: _____

Date: _____

The words below describe different groups of things. Match the words with the group names.

Go to:

http://www.infoseek.com/Facts?pg=deskref.html

geese	**seagulls**
quail	**fish**
grapes	**elephants**
whales	

1. A cluster of _____ makes an excellent snack.

2. The herd of _____ began chasing away the lion.

3. A pod of _____ swam under the ship.

4. The gaggle of _____ flew south for the winter.

5. A large school of _____ came toward my hook.

6. The flock of _____ rested on the beach.

7. A small covey of _____ ran under the brush.

AMAZING MAZES

Objective(s):

Students will...

- use geometry and spatial sense to navigate through a series of mazes.
- research information about the mythical Minotaur and his maze.
- construct a maze.

Materials Needed:

- computer
- student activity sheet

Web Site(s):

- http://www.wln.com/~deltapac/maze/mazepage.html
- http://www.wln.com/~deltapac/maze/maze_2.html
- http://www.wln.com/~deltapac/maze/mazelett.html
- http://www.altavista.com
- http://www.yahoo.com

Teaching the Lesson:

These lessons are all complementary to each other or any geometry-related topic. Students will enjoy navigating through the mazes. Since it is competitive, they will use their sense of geometrical order to move as quickly as possible. In addition, they will create their own mazes in order to challenge their friends. Be sure this is not too complex; they can get carried away! The section on the Minotaur legend is a great jumping-off point to learn about Greek or other myths and legends.

NCTM Standards: 1, 2, 3, 4, 5, 6, 9, 13

AMAZING MAZES

Name: _____

Date: _____

Go to:

http://www.wln.com/~deltapac/maze/mazepage.html

Read the directions on the page to use the maze puzzles.

1. Find your way through the maze. Have a partner time how long it takes you to go in one direction. How long did it take you?

   _____

2. Now, time your partner. How long did it take your partner?

   _____

3. How long did it take you to go from the top of the maze to the bottom of the maze?

   _____

4. How long did it take to go from the bottom to the top?

   _____

5. How did your partner do on the maze? Was he or she faster or slower than you through the maze? Why do you think this happened?

   _____

   _____

   _____

   _____

AMAZING MAZES *(cont.)*

Name: _____

Date: _____

Prepare yourself for another maze challenge!

Go to:

http://www.wln.com/~deltapac/maze/maze_2.html

Follow the directions to play the maze game.

1. Have a partner time how long it takes for you to get through the maze. Then, write this information down.

   _____

2. Now time how long it takes for your partner to get through the maze. Then, write this information down.

   _____

3. Compare your time through the maze with your partner's time. Do you think watching someone else go through the maze helps you to get through faster?

   _____

4. Can you think of some things in real life that are like a maze?

   _____

   _____

   _____

   _____

   _____

AMAZING MAZES *(cont.)*

Name: _____

Date: _____

Go to:

http://www.wln.com/~deltapac/maze/mazelett.html

Working alone or with a partner, try to discover the secret message as you complete your way around the maze. Write down the secret message below. Be sure that you start at the top, or your message will be backwards!

_____

In Greek mythology, a nasty creature known as the Minotaur challenged humans to try to run through his labyrinth, or maze to us. Use the Internet to look up information about the myth of the Minotaur and his maze.

Go to:

http://www.altavista.com

or

http://www.yahoo.com

Type the word Minotaur in the box and click on the Search button.

When you have found enough information, write a paragraph below about the legend of the Minotaur and his maze.

_____

_____

_____

_____

_____

_____

AMAZING MAZES *(cont.)*

Name: _____

Date: _____

Draw your own maze in the space below. Challenge your partner to solve your maze, and you should try to solve his or hers.

SAME-SIDED SAMENESS

Objective(s):

Students will...

- identify characteristics of symmetry.

Materials Needed:

- computer
- student activity sheet

Web Site(s):

- http://www.sirius.com/~fonzilla/swllwtl.jpg
- http://www.sirius.com/~fonzilla/bug47.gif
- http://www.mykoweb.com/BAF/species/Geastrum_fornicatum.html

Teaching the Lesson:

This lesson helps students to find symmetry (in this case, bilateral symmetry) in various living things. Teach the overall patterns of symmetry in the living and non-living world along with this lesson. Also, discuss whether symmetry is the exception or the rule in the world around us.

NCTM Standards: 1, 2, 3, 4, 9, 13

SAME-SIDED SAMENESS

Name: _____

Date: _____

Think about your arms and legs, your ears and eyes, your fingers and toes. There are the same number on both sides of your body—one arm and one leg on each side, one ear and one eye, and so on. This is called symmetry. Something that has symmetry on both sides of it is called symmetrical.

Write down the names of five symmetrical things in the first column below. In the second column, write down the names of five things that are not symmetrical. For example, a door has a handle only on one side.

_____   _____

_____   _____

_____   _____

_____   _____

_____   _____

Go to:

http://www.sirius.com/~fonzilla/swllwtl.jpg

Are you looking at something symmetrical? Explain why or why not.

_____

Go to:

http://www.sirius.com/~fonzilla/bug47.gif

Is this creature symmetrical? How do you know?

_____

Go to:

http://www.mykoweb.com/BAF/species/Geastrum_fornicatum.html

Are these funguses symmetrical? Why or why not?

_____

_____

RADICAL RADIAL SYMMETRY

Objective(s):

Students will...

- identify objects that possess the property of radial symmetry.

Materials Needed:

- computer
- student activity sheet

Web Site(s):

- http://www.hedgerows.com/UBCBotGdn/

Teaching the Lesson:

Radial symmetry is more difficult to teach than bilateral symmetry (or 'regular' symmetry). It is important, therefore, to consider bringing in materials such as flowers, dried sea stars, sea urchins, and other living and non-living things that possess this property. You might want to have the students discuss or write a short paper on what people would look like if they were radially symmetrical and how things would be different for them. Drawing would be fun, too!

NCTM Standards: 1, 2, 3, 4, 9, 13

RADICAL RADIAL SYMMETRY

Name: _____

Date: _____

Sometimes things are symmetrical even if they have are not really even on both sides. For instance, a bicycle wheel is symmetrical because the spokes all come out the same way from the center of the wheel. Another example is a flower.

Go to:

http://www.hedgerows.com/UBCBotGdn/

Make a list of five things that are the same all the way around like the flower you see on your screen.

_____

_____

_____

_____

_____

SIGNS SHAPE UP

Objective(s):

Students will...

- identify shapes in traffic signs and their characteristics.
- construct their own traffic signs.

Materials Needed:

- computer
- student activity sheet
- construction paper
- scissors
- crayons
- ruler

Web Site(s):

- http://www.dmv.ca.gov/hdbk/dl600(pg19).htm#WrnSigns
- http://www.ampsc.com/~engage/htm/WarSigns.html
- http://www.ampsc.com/~engage/htm/RegSigns.html

Teaching the Lesson:

Introduce this topic with a discussion of what would happen if no one could tell one traffic sign from the other or if we didn't have them at all. Emphasize quality of work when they design their own signs.

NCTM Standards: 2, 3, 4, 9, 10, 13

SIGNS SHAPE UP

Name: _____

Date: _____

Go to:

http://www.dmv.ca.gov/hdbk/dl600(pg19).htm#WrnSigns

Answer the following questions about the traffic signs on this page.

1. What shape are the yellow signs?

   _____

2. What is the shape of the sign that reads "left turn yield on green"?

   _____

3. What is the shape of the "speed limit 55" sign?

   _____

4. What shape is the blue "next service 22 miles" sign?

   _____

SIGNS SHAPE UP *(cont.)*

Name: _____

Date: _____

Go to:

http://www.ampsc.com/~engage/htm/WarSigns.html

1. There are two signs in this group that are NOT squares. Put the cursor (you don't need to click) on each sign and write down what each means.

_____

Go to:

http://www.ampsc.com/~engage/htm/RegSigns.html

2. Draw a picture of the sign that is made of TWO rectangles.

3. What is the name of the sign that has SIX sides?

_____

4. Find the sign that has THREE sides. Draw a picture of it.

SIGNS SHAPE UP *(cont.)*

Name: _____

Date: _____

Pretend that you are a road engineer. Your job is to make the highways and roads safe for people to travel on. Today is your day to design five new signs. They should each say something or be a symbol of safety.

Go to:

http://www.ampsc.com/~engage/htm/WarSigns.html

You can find some ideas at this Web page, but do not copy. Each sign must be your own design. Use the following shapes in your signs:

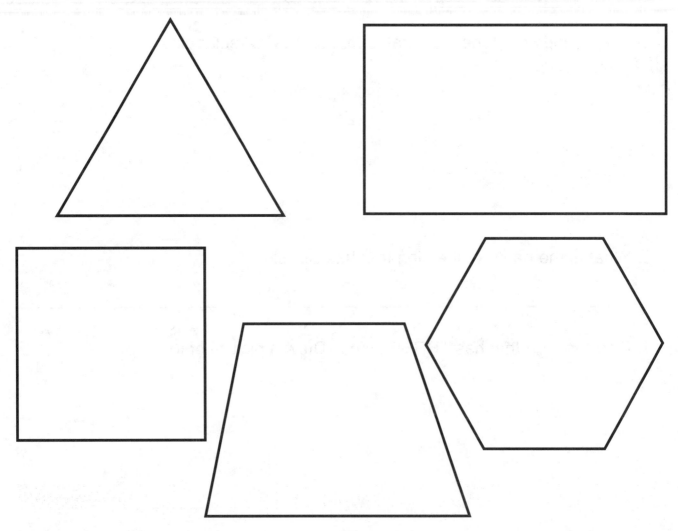

UNDER THE SEA

Objective(s):

Students will...

- interact with the Web site and match patterns and shapes.
- write a short story describing an undersea experience.

Materials Needed:

- computer
- student activity sheet

Web Site(s):

- http://www.ctw.org/preschool/games/play/0,1167,1286,00.html

Teaching the Lesson:

Lower-level students will appreciate this special chance at shape recognition. Use the short story as a springboard to discuss and learn about diving under the sea and how things appear differently under water from the way they do on land.

NCTM Standards: 2, 4, 9, 13

UNDER THE SEA

Name: _____

Date: _____

Go to:

http://www.ctw.org/preschool/games/play/0,1167,1286,00.html

Play the game. Find the matching shapes. When you are finished, what does Betty Lou do?

_____

Now draw three more shapes of things you would like to see if you were going skin diving with Betty Lou.

Write a paragraph about your adventure with Betty Lou under the sea.

_____

_____

_____

FISHBOWL FROLIC

Objective(s):

Students will...

- create a geometric pattern by connecting the dots online.

Materials Needed:

- computer
- student activity sheet

Web Site(s):

- http://www.ctw.org/preschool/games/play/0,1167,1467,00.html

Teaching the Lesson:

Connecting the dots seems simple, but for some students it is complicated enough. Have students discuss the "shape" of a fishbowl. Can they describe a fishbowl without using the word fishbowl?

NCTM Standards: 4, 9, 13

FISHBOWL FROLIC

Name: _____

Date: _____

Go to:

http://www.ctw.org/preschool/games/play/0,1167,1467,00.html

Play the game by connecting the dots.

1. What did you make when you finished?

   _____

2. Why do you think fishbowls are shaped that way?

   _____

3. Draw two more fishbowls that are not shaped like most other fishbowls. Be sure to draw the fish inside!

IT TAKES A TRAINED EYE

Objective(s):

Students will...

- recognize pattern differences and similarities in trains.

Materials Needed:

- computer
- student activity sheet

Web Site(s):

- http://www.trainsaregood.com/ertl.htm

Teaching the Lesson:

This is a good time to introduce the idea that the perception of differences depends on how closely one looks for them. For example, students cannot tell one antelope from another in a herd, but the antelopes can identify one another. Searching for and identifying details is a skill they should continue to practice beyond this lesson.

NCTM Standards: 1, 2, 3, 4, 9, 13

IT TAKES A TRAINED EYE

Name: _____

Date: _____

Go to:

http://www.trainsaregood.com/ertl.htm

On this page are pictures of several different train engines. Pick three engines and describe each one. Be sure to include color, size, number of wheels, and anything unique about the engine.

Engine 1
Name: _____

_____

_____

_____

Engine 2
Name: _____

_____

_____

_____

Engine 3
Name: _____

_____

_____

_____

The engines are different in some ways. They are different colors, they have a different number of wheels, some are smiling, some are not. What do the three engines have in common with each other that lets you know they are all trains?

_____

_____

SPOT THE SHAPE

Objective(s):

Students will...

- search for patterns of symmetry and create their own.
- identify shapes contained in those patterns.

Materials Needed:

- computer
- student activity sheet

Web Site(s):

- http://www.jcdi-online.com/allq.html
- http://www.nmia.com/~mgdesign/moosing.gif

Teaching the Lesson:

Use these lessons to supplement others in this book about symmetry and pattern recognition. The students should be introduced to the concept of symmetry and might be made aware of symmetrical things they may already depend on, such as when making small hearts or paper dolls by folding paper in half.

NCTM Standards: 4, 9, 13

SPOT THE SHAPE

Name: _____

Date: _____

Go to:

http://www.jcdi-online.com/allq.html

Look carefully at all the patterns on this Web page. Imagine folding each of them in half. Symmetry means that if you fold something in half, it will be the same on both sides. Pick out the patterns that have symmetry and those that do not. Write down the names of each on the chart below.

Has Symmetry	No Symmetry

SPOT THE SHAPE *(cont.)*

Name: _____

Date: _____

Go to:

http://www.nmia.com/~mgdesign/moosing.gif

Find the orange section of the quilt pattern (without the cow in it).

1. How many squares do you see?

_____

2. How many small triangles can you see?

_____

3. How many large triangles can you see?

_____

Now find the purple section of the quilt pattern.

4. How many light purple squares are there?

_____

5. How many dark purple squares do you see?

_____

SPOT THE SHAPE *(cont.)*

Name: _____

Date: _____

Go to:

http://www.nmia.com/~mgdesign/moosing.gif

Find the green part of the quilt pattern (without the cow).

1. How many dark green triangles are there?

_____

2. How many light green triangles are there?

_____

3. How many light and dark green triangles can be put together to make a square?

_____

4. How many squares are there?

_____

5. If the dark green triangles disappeared, how many squares could be made from the remaining triangles?

_____

THE HANDS OF TIME

Objective(s):

Students will...

- tell time using analog and digital watches.

Materials Needed:

- computer
- student activity sheets

Web Site(s):

- http://www.timex.com/cgi-bin/display?product=22522
- http://www.timex.com/cgi-bin/display?product=77517

Teaching the Lesson:

These activities are supplements to a time-related unit. It is a good opportunity to discuss the topic of digital v. analog watches. Some students may prefer one over the other for various reasons. A short discussion/debate about the merits of each style can be integrated into this topic also.

NCTM Standards: 1, 2, 3, 4, 9, 13

THE HANDS OF TIME

Name: _____

Date: _____

Go to:

http://www.timex.com/cgi-bin/display?product=22522

Directions: Use the picture found here to answer the questions below.

1. What is the exact time?

   _____

2. What hour in the day is it?

   _____

3. How many minutes have passed in the hour?

   _____

4. How many seconds have passed in the minute?

   _____

5. Can you tell from this watch whether it is morning or night?

   _____

THE HANDS OF TIME *(cont.)*

Name: _____

Date: _____

Go to:

http://www.timex.com/cgi-bin/display?product=77517

Directions: Look carefully at the picture on this Web page. Answer the questions below.

1. What time is it according to the watch?

   _____

2. Is it morning or night? (You will have to look carefully to find out.)

   _____

3. How many minutes have passed in the hour?

   _____

4. How many seconds have passed in the minute?

   _____

5. Do you think this kind of watch is easier or harder to read than a watch with hands? Why?

   _____

   _____

WHAT TIME DO YOU HAVE?

Objective(s):

Students will...

- use cues in the images on this Web page to determine time of day and other aspects of the passage of time.

Materials Needed:

- computer
- student activity sheet

Web Site(s):

- http://www.xmission.com/~emailbox/cyberkitty.htm

Teaching the Lesson:

In this lesson, students should be familiar with telling time and know that certain events in life occur on a regular schedule. You can use this lesson as a springboard to find out if students have a particular schedule of their own, (usually set by parents) such as when to go to bed, when to get up, etc.

NCTM Standards: 1, 2, 3, 4, 6, 13

WHAT TIME DO YOU HAVE?

Name: _____

Date: _____

Go to:

http://www.xmission.com/~emailbox/cyberkitty.htm

1. Find the clock. What time does the clock say?

   _____

2. Look at the window. Do you think the clock is showing morning or evening hours?

   _____

3. Find the picture of the kitty brush. How often do you think cats should be brushed?

   _____

4. What are two things that you do in the morning but do not do at night?

   _____

YOUR SCHEDULE

Objective(s):

Students will...

- use their knowledge of time concepts to create a schedule for themselves.

Materials Needed:

- computer
- student activity sheet

Web Site(s):

- http://www.timex.com/

Teaching the Lesson:

The students should be introduced to the concepts of time schedules prior to this activity. The reasons for scheduling their time for structure may be a new idea for many of them. However, it is a good habit to instill at this age. Furthermore, a post activity discussion can explore ways to create and store schedules, such as PDAs, etc.

NCTM Standards: 1, 2, 3, 4, 6, 13

YOUR SCHEDULE

Name: _____

Date: _____

Everyone has certain things that he or she does on a regular schedule. For instance, you probably arrive at school at the same time every day. Try to think of four or five things that you do at about the same time every day. Then write down a schedule for yourself, using the table below.

	What I Do:	**What Time I Do It:**
Example	get up from bed	7:15 A.M.

Go to:

http://www.timex.com/

1. Click one of the links to find a watch that you like, and then draw a picture of it below.

2. What is the name of the watch that you chose?

_____

3. Next, draw a picture of what the watch would look like at each time during the day based on your schedule above.

DON'T RUN OUT

Objective(s):

Students will...

- determine if the battery power in a CD player is sufficient for a predetermined time period of play.

Materials Needed:

- computer
- student activity sheet

Web Site(s):

- http://www.philipsstores.com/shpa49.html

Teaching the Lesson:

In this activity, students need to be prepared to do some simple calculations to determine the answer to the time-related questions. Explore the possibilities with them after the lesson to find out what else could be done besides waiting for the batteries to run down.

NCTM Standards: 1, 2, 3, 4, 6, 7, 8, 13

DON'T RUN OUT

Name: _____

Date: _____

You have just been given a new personal compact disc player for your birthday!

Go to:

http://www.philipsstores.com/shpa49.html

Let's see what it looks like and get information to answer the questions below.

On a nine-hour trip across the state to see your grandparents, you listen to your CD player in the car. You have brought nine compact discs for your listening enjoyment. Each disc is one hour long.

1. How long do you need your batteries to last if you want to listen to all of your CDs?

   _____

   _____

2. How long should your batteries last according to the information on the Internet?

   _____

   _____

3. If you want to listen to your CDs again on the way home, do you have enough battery power left?

   _____

   _____

IT'S TV TIME

Objective(s):

Students will...

- create a schedule using TV listings.

Materials Needed:

- computer
- student activity sheet

Web Site(s):

- http://www.wmht.org/kids/schedule.htm

Teaching the Lesson:

Students will enjoy the idea of watching TV all day. This serves as a point of discussion to supplement the questions about TV habits at the end of this lesson. If the choices of TV programs are not to your liking, another set of listings can be found at

- http://www.tvgen.com/

NCTM Standards: 2, 3, 4, 6, 11, 13

IT'S TV TIME

Name: _____

Date: _____

Your good friend Stacey has tonsilitis. Her tonsils have to be taken out and she will be in the hospital one entire night and day. Stacey will be too tired after the surgery to read any books, so she will have to watch television the whole day in the hospital. As her good friend, you have volunteered to help her make a schedule of television shows that might help her feel better.

Your assignment is to write out a TV time schedule for Stacey.

Go to:

http://www.wmht.org/kids/schedule.htm

Write out a time schedule for her. Fill in the shows she will watch during the day and evening. Remember to fill in things like breakfast, lunch, and dinner, too.

Time	Name of Show
8:00 A.M.	
8:30 A.M.	
9:00 A.M.	
9:30 A.M.	
10:00 A.M.	
10:30 A.M.	
11:00 A.M.	
11:30 M.	
12:00 P.M.	
12:30 P.M.	

IT'S TV TIME *(cont.)*

Name: _____

Date: _____

Time	Name of Show
1:00 P.M.	
1:30 P.M.	
2:00 P.M.	
2:30 P.M.	
3:00 P.M.	
3:30 P.M.	
4:00 P.M.	
4:30 P.M.	
5:00 P.M.	
5:30 P.M.	
6:00 P.M.	
6:30 P.M.	
7:00 P.M.	
7:30 P.M.	
8:00 P.M.	

How many hours of televsion do you watch each day?

_____

Do you think you watch too much television?

_____

How many books do you read in a week?

_____

Do you think that you read enough books?

_____

BILLS, BILLS, BILLS

Objective(s):

Students will...

- examine patterns and relationships.
- complete whole-number operations.

Materials Needed:

- student activity sheet
- computer

Web Site(s):

- http://www.ustreas.gov/currency/

Teaching the Lesson:

In this activity, the students may become curious about just who these people are that appear on our paper money. Be prepared to answer questions about who your students will see on the money. As an extension, use this as a jumping-off point for a history lesson on the important people on our bills.

BILLS, BILLS, BILLS

Name: _____

Date: _____

Go to:

http://www.ustreas.gov/currency/

Write down the name of the person whose face appears on the following bills:

1 dollar _____

2 dollar _____

5 dollar _____

10 dollar _____

20 dollar _____

50 dollar _____

100 dollar _____

Add together the value of bills with the following names:

one Jackson + one Washington + one Franklin = _____

one Grant + one Hamilton + two Lincolns = _____

two Jacksons + one Jefferson + one Grant = _____

MAKE YOUR OWN FUNNY MONEY

Objective(s):

Students will...

- learn what other forms of money look like.
- construct their own "funny" money.

Materials Needed:

- student activity sheet
- computer
- scissors
- construction paper
- ruler

Web Site(s):

- http://www.ease.com/~randyj/money1.htm
- http://www.treas.gov/kids/money/detect.html

Teaching the Lesson:

Students should be given a preview about the money of other countries and told that every country places important historical figures on their money. They should be given a wide berth on how they design their money. After they are done, post the bills on the board for all to see. The extension activity should be used as an enrichment activitiy and can be a part of a unit on government, crime, or technology. A class discussion would be appropriate, as well, on this topic.

MAKE YOUR OWN FUNNY MONEY

Name: _____

Date: _____

Money always has pictures of important people or things on it. Some countries use presidents, others use kings and queens, and some have pictures of important places on it. You are an important person, so why not make some money with a picture of you on it? Here is your chance.

Go to:

http://www.ease.com/~randyj/money1.htm

Here you will find some ideas about what money from different countries looks like. Then design two bills. One will be worth 1 dollar, the other worth 100 dollars. Draw the fronts and backsides of these bills. Then cut them out and glue the fronts and backsides together. Compare with your friends. Your teacher will post everyone's money on the bulletin board!

Extension: How does the United States try to stop people from making counterfeit (fake) money? This Web site has some information about this topic.

Go to:

http://www.treas.gov/kids/money/detect.html

WILL THE REAL COIN PLEASE STAND UP?

Objective(s):

Students will...

- identify subtle differences among coins to find the "real" one.
- draw their own coins.
- try to create a coin group in which a real coin is concealed.

Materials Needed:

- computer
- student activity sheet

Web Site(s):

- http://www.exploratorium.edu/memory/index.html

Teaching the Lesson:

This lesson can serve to show how tiny differences which are not normally taken into account can be very significant. Pattern recognition-related activities serve as a good supplement to this topic, as well as introducing topics such as numismatics, rare and unusual coins, and even counterfeiting.

NCTM Standards: 1, 2, 3, 4, 9, 13

WILL THE REAL COIN PLEASE STAND UP?

Name: _____

Date: _____

Go to:

http://www.exploratorium.edu/memory/index.html

Find out which coin is the real one! Without clicking on any coin, look them all over carefully. Write down which one you think is the "real" coin.

_____

Next, explain why the other coins do not seem like the right one.

_____

_____

_____

Now, check your answer! Click on the coin that you think is the "real" coin. Were you right? Why or why not?

_____

_____

_____

Next, using a different coin, draw three coins below. Only one of them should look like the real coin. The others should be slightly different. Challenge your partner to find the "real" coin.

SHOP TILL YOU DROP

Objective(s):

Students will...

- decide on appropriate products to purchase.
- determine their prices.
- compute the total amount spent.

Materials Needed:

- student activity sheet
- computer

Web Site(s):

- http://www.eddiebauer.com
- http://www.etoys.com/
- http://www.candydirect.com/cgi-bin/sc.pl?status=index&ip=traino
- http://www.damark.com

Teaching the Lesson:

You may need to help students get oriented on the Web sites, showing them how to search for a particular product, if needed. Emphasize that they should keep a running total of their purchases so they do not go over their limit.

NCTM Standards: 1, 2, 4, 5, 6, 12

SHOP TILL YOU DROP

Name: _____

Date: _____

You've just won $1,000 in a telephone survey contest! To keep the money, you must spend it all right now on the Internet. You must come within $25 of the $1,000 you have just won. You have to buy between five and 15 items that total at least $975. Are you up to the challenge?

Choose one of the links below and find 15 items or fewer. Add up the prices to be sure that you follow the contest rules.

Go to:

http://www.eddiebauer.com
http://www.etoys.com/
http://www.candydirect.com/cgi-bin/sc.pl?status=index&ip=traino
http://www.damark.oom

What I Bought:	Where I Bought It:	Price:
_____	_____	_____
_____	_____	_____
_____	_____	_____
_____	_____	_____
_____	_____	_____
_____	_____	_____
_____	_____	_____
_____	_____	_____
_____	_____	_____
_____	_____	_____
_____	_____	_____
_____	_____	_____
_____	_____	_____
_____	_____	_____

Total Price for all items: _____

Did you win? _____

TICKET TO RIDE

Objective(s):

Students will...

- apply measurement information to determine their eligibility to get on an amusement park ride.

Materials Needed:

- computer
- student activity sheet
- ruler or yardstick

Web Site(s):

- http://www.kennywood.com/rides.html

Teaching the Lesson:

Students will really enjoy going on an imaginary amusement park trip and seeing how "unfair" some of the rules are! A very important extension to this activity is to examine how height restrictions are determined and why these rules are necessary. The writing assignment will generate lots of opinions too!

NCTM Standards: 1, 2, 3, 4, 5, 6, 7, 8, 10, 13

TICKET TO RIDE

Name: _____

Date: _____

Aren't you lucky? You have been invited along with your classmates to an amusement park with all sorts of fun rides. You will spend all day there, and the planning has already begun! What will you eat? What games will you play? Then suddenly someone says, "You know, on some of the rides, you have to be above a certain height to get on the ride." You need to do some research before the trip and find out the following information.

Go to:

http://www.kennywood.com/rides.html

Will you get to ride? Check the Web site for the height rules on at least five different rides you are interested in.

Minimum height:	**Name of Ride**
_____	_____
_____	_____
_____	_____
_____	_____
_____	_____

Using a yardstick, have a partner help you measure your height in inches. Then help your partner do the same.

What is your height?_____

What is your partner's height? _____

Which rides will you be able to go on?_____

_____

Write a paragraph about why you think people have to be above a certain height to get on some rides. Do you think this is fair? Why or why not?

JUNGLE AND OCEAN

Objective(s):

Students will...

- gather and analyze numerical data on elephants and sharks.

Materials Needed:

- computer
- student activity sheet

Web Site(s):

- http://library.advanced.org/11922/african/elephants.htm
- http://www.cybervault.com/users/D/dgrgich/picshark.html
- http://www.cybervault.com/users/D/dgrgich/txtshrk.html

Teaching the Lesson:

This lesson might be used to introduce, supplement, or review the idea of analyzing numerical data from sources to find out useful information. You should mention that information like this may be of use in a future book report. Students can continue this topic for practice and find out a great deal more regarding elephants and sharks and analyze information to reach a conclusion. For example, researching information about the numbers of elephants poached for the past 25 years and looking for a trend would be an excellent extension.

NCTM Standards: 1, 2, 3, 4, 6, 9, 10, 13

JUNGLE AND OCEAN

Name: _____

Date: _____

Elephants are the largest animals living on land today. Let's find out more about them!

Go to:

http://library.advanced.org/11922/african/elephants.htm

1. How long is the elephant's tail?

   _____

2. How tall do they stand?

   _____

3. How many pounds of vegetation do they eat each day?

   _____

4. How much can an elephant weigh?

   _____

5. How many hind-foot toes are there on an African elephant?

   _____

90

JUNGLE AND OCEAN *(cont.)*

Name: _____

Date: _____

Go to:

http://www.cybervault.com/users/D/dgrgich/picshark.html

1. What is the size range of the great white shark in feet?

_____

2. What is the size range of the great white shark in meters?

_____

Go to:

http://www.cybervault.com/users/D/dgrgich/txtshrk.html

3. How many people are killed each year by great white shark attacks?

_____

4. How fast can sharks swim?

_____

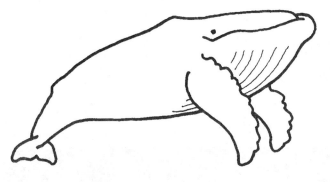

FROM HERE TO THERE

Objective(s)

Students will...

- determine the distances and travel times related to a cross country automobile trip.

Materials Needed:

- computer
- student activity sheet

Web Site(s):

- http://www.mapquest.com/

Teaching the Lesson:

This is another lesson that allows students to apply a variety of skills as they complete it. Be sure that they follow the directions on the Web page carefully to navigate through the trip calculator. Again, these activities provide a strong foundation for any related subjects such as transportation and history, as well as more mathematics opportunities.

NCTM Standards: 1, 2, 3, 4, 6, 7, 8, 10, 12, 13

FROM HERE TO THERE

Name: _____

Date: _____

Suppose you are going to take a trip from Los Angeles, California to Prescott, Arizona. You are going to start at Los Angeles City Hall and stop at the Prescott City Hall. Use the Internet to help you find the fastest way to get there.

Directions:

Go to:

http://www.mapquest.com/

When you are there, you should...

- click on "tripquest."
- select city-to-city.
- use the menu bar on the page to select "City Hall."
- type in Los Angeles where it says "city" and CA where it says "state" as your starting point. Use Prescott and AZ as your destination.
- click "calculate directions" at the bottom of the page.

1. What distance will you travel on the Hollywood Freeway?

   _____

2. How many miles will you travel east on I-10 to Arizona?

   _____

3. How far will you drive northeast on State Route 71 to State Route 89?

   _____

4. What will be the total distance on this trip?

   _____

FROM HERE TO THERE *(cont.)*

Name: _____

Date: _____

Imagine that this summer you are going to visit Disneyland in Anaheim, California, and drive to Disneyworld in Orlando, Florida, to see which one you like better. Use the Internet to help you find the fastest way to reach your destination.

Go to

http://www.mapquest.com

- Click on tripquest.
- Select city-to-city for your route type.
- For your starting point, select "Amusement Parks" on the menu bar.
- Type in Anaheim for the city, and CA for the state.
- For your destination, select "Amusement Parks" on the menu bar and type Orlando for the city. Then type FL for the state.
- At the bottom of the page, click "calculate directions."

1. How many miles will you travel on State Route 60 to I-10?

   _____

2. What distance will you drive on I-10 to Lousiana?

   _____

3. How many miles will you travel in the state of Alabama?

   _____

4. What is the total distance of your trip?

   _____

TALLER THAN THE TALLEST TREE

Objective(s):

Students will...

- research and record numerical data on the world's tallest trees.

Materials Needed:

- computer
- student activity sheet

Web Site(s):

- http://www.nps.gov/redw/sequoias.htm

Teaching the Lesson:

Use this activity to bring out in students a sense of awe and wonder about some of earth's oldest and largest living things. You can extend this activity by comparing some of the statistics with things that students are familiar with, such as the height of the school building.

NCTM Standards: 1, 2, 3, 4, 6, 7, 10, 13

TALLER THAN THE TALLEST TREE

Name: _____

Date: _____

Go to:

http://www.nps.gov/redw/sequoias.htm

Directions: Use the information on this Web page to answer the questions below about the giant redwood tree.

1. How tall is the tallest redwood tree?

   _____

2. How much can this tree weigh?

   _____

3. How old is it?

   _____

4. Write a paragraph about the things that the tree may have "seen" through its lifetime until today.

   _____

   _____

   _____

   _____

   _____

ZOO TOUR

Objective(s):

Students will...

- solve a mystery by using information on the Internet.

Materials Needed:

- computer
- student activity sheet

Web Site(s):

- http://library.advanced.org/11922/

Teaching the Lesson:

This lesson lends itself to group or individual work. It is designed to help students apply many of the skills they have learned in one activity. Be sure to allot at least two class periods to complete it. They should be asked to keep a record of their progress through the "zoo" so they don't lose their way.

NCTM Standards: 1, 2, 3, 4, 6, 7, 8, 9, 10, 11, 13

ZOO TOUR

Name: _____

Date: _____

Go to:

http://library.advanced.org/11922/

Take a careful look at the map of the virtual zoo. One of the reptiles has escaped! To find out which one, click on the reptile house on the map and answer these questions:

1. It is a reptile that spends much of its time in the water. The choices are

   _____

   _____

   _____

2. This reptile also has its own "house" that it uses for protection. What is the name of the escaped reptile?

   _____

After you have written the name of the escaped reptile, click on its name. Then read the information about it and answer the following questions.

3. How small is the smallest and how large is the largest of this escaped reptile?

   _____

4. How long can these animals live?

   _____

5. How many different species (kinds) of these animals are in danger of being extinct?

   _____

Click the "back" button when you finish this question.

ZOO TOUR *(cont.)*

Name: _____

Date: _____

Now let's try to find the escaped reptile!

We know that he can't move very fast, so we have a good chance of catching him and returning him to his home in the reptile house.

He just got out of the water, so he left a good trail of drips behind him. First, he went ten yards straight to the extinct animals! Then he turned right and went another five yards to visit the small mammals.

1. How far has our escaped friend travelled so far?

_____

His next journey was a long one. The reptile walked up and to the left for 20 yards and stopped at the bears for a rest. After his rest, our friend cruised down to the African animals, which was a distance of another 15 yards.

2. What is the distance from the small mammals to the African animals?

_____

The tracks stopped right where the lions are kept! What happened to our friend? Wait, you see a few tracks going toward monkey island, seven yards away. Better hurry, those tracks are drying up.

3. How far has the escaped reptile travelled since he was at the bears?

_____

As you look toward monkey island, you see the monkeys chattering wildly and pointing toward the water. There, on a floating log, is your long-lost reptile!

4. How far must you walk to get back to the reptile house with the escaped reptile?

_____

ZOO TOUR *(cont.)*

Name: _____

Date: _____

Since you solved the mystery of the missing turtle, the zookeepers want to give you a grand tour of the rest of the zoo! You decide at once that you would like to visit the pandas, which is only ten yards from the reptile house where you dropped off the escaped turtle.

Click on the panda paradise!

1. How many pictures of pandas do you see?

   _____

Click the "back" button when you finish this question.

After your wonderful visit with the pandas, the zookeepers offer to take you to see the ocean life at the zoo, just five yards from the pandas.

2. How far have you travelled from the reptile house so far?

   _____

Click on the ocean life!

3. How many "swimming" fish do you see at the top of the page?

   _____

4. How many species (kinds) of fish live in the world?

   _____

5. What fraction of fish live in fresh water?

   _____

6. Water makes up what percentage of the world's surface?

   _____

Click the "back" button when you finish this question.

ZOO TOUR *(cont.)*

Name: _____

Date: _____

Time to visit the birds! They are in the amazing aviary, only three yards from the ocean animals. Click on the amazing aviary. You have such a variety of birds to look at! Let's click on the hummingbird.

7. How small is the smallest kind of hummingbird, the bee hummingbird?

   _____

8. How many eggs do hummingbirds lay?

   _____

Click the "back" button when you finish this question.

It is time to start home from the tour of the zoo. You wish you had time to stop and visit more of the animals, but the day is at an end.

9. Which is the fastest way back to the reptile house so you can say goodbye before you leave?

10. Will you walk five yards to the monkey island and go around toward the bears? Or will you go back toward the ocean animals and reach the reptile house going that way?

Work out the problem, using the rest of this page. Be sure to write the distances from place to place in one direction and then the next. Add up the total distance and decide which is the fastest way to the reptile house! Good luck!

_____

_____

_____

_____

WEATHER OR NOT

Objective(s):

Students will...

- examine weather predictions and record information.
- analyze data that compares the weather of one region in the world to another.

Materials Needed:

- computer
- student activity sheet

Web Site(s):

- http://www.weather.com/weather/int/
- http://www.intellicast.com/weather/usa/

Teaching the Lesson:

For variety, you can have students input data from other regions of the world and come up with a classroom chart that compares a broader range of world climates. This is a good place to introduce weather, the ideas behind predictions, and weather technology.

NCTM Standards: 1, 2, 3, 4, 5, 9, 10, 11, 12, 13

WEATHER OR NOT

Name: _____

Date: _____

Go to:

http://www.weather.com/weather/int/

Find out what the weather is like in London, England, right now. Type "London" in the blank where is says "city." Then read the information very carefully.

1. What is the temperature today in London?

   _____

2. Is it windy?

   _____

3. What is the relative humidity?

   _____

4. What kind of weather is forecast (predicted) for the next three days?

   Day one: _____

   _____

   Day two: _____

   _____

   Day three: _____

   _____

WEATHER OR NOT *(cont.)*

Name: _____

Date: _____

Go to:

http://www.intellicast.com/weather/usa/

Directions: Follow the directions below and answer the questions to guide you through this Web site.

Click on "High Temps."

1. What is the highest temperature going to be in the U.S. today?

Return to the first page by clicking the "back" button.

Click on "Low Temps."

2. What will be the lowest temperature in the U.S. today?

_____

3. What is the difference between the highest and lowest of the "high" temperatures?

_____

4. What is the difference between the highest and lowest "low" temperatures?

_____

_____

     104

WE ALL SCREAM FOR ICE CREAM

Objective(s):

Students will...

- conduct a survey, graph the results, and compare them to the results of a similar survey on the Internet.

Materials Needed:

- computer
- student activity sheet

Web Site(s):

- http://www.kent.pvt.k12.ct.us/students/oneils/ice.htm

Teaching the Lesson:

You will probably need to organize the survey. Go over some bar graph skills with students prior to this activity. They should also be comfortable reading a pie graph. This activity can be used to show students that things they are interested in are interesting to other people too, and sometimes are studied scientifically. Note that the Internet survey had an "other" category for flavors, and you may wish to include that in your class survey.

You should also talk about sample size and the accuracy of a survey before this lesson.

NCTM Standards: 1, 2, 3, 4, 6, 7, 9, 10, 11, 12, 13

WE ALL SCREAM FOR ICE CREAM

Name: _____

Date: _____

You are in charge of buying the ice cream for a birthday party with all your classmates. Before buying any ice cream, you need to decide which kind to buy. You have enough money for five containers of ice cream and have decided that you will buy chocolate, vanilla and strawberry. But how much of each flavor will you buy?

The best way to find out is to do a survey in class. Your teacher will ask the class to vote on their favorite of the three flavors. Fill in the chart below.

Flavor	Number of Votes
chocolate	_____
vanilla	_____
strawberry	_____

It is useful to graph a survey like this so that you can see a picture of which ice cream is liked the most and which ice cream is liked the least. Fill in the graph below. For each flavor in your survey, graph the number of people who liked that flavor the best.

	Chocolate	Vanilla	Strawberry
30			
25			
20			
15			
10			
5			
0			

WE ALL SCREAM FOR ICE CREAM *(cont.)*

Name: _____

Date: _____

Now let's find out if the kids in your class like the same kinds of ice cream as the rest of the people in the United States.

Go to:

http://www.kent.pvt.k12.ct.us/students/oneils/ice.htm

1. What do you suppose "other" means on the pie graph shown at this Web site?

   _____

2. Just by looking at the size of each "piece" of the graph, you can tell what the favorite flavors were. List the favorite flavors of Americans.

   _____

   _____

   _____

3. How did your survey compare with the one on the Internet? Were your class favorites the same or different from those on the Internet survey?

   _____

   _____

Bonus: Make a list of five "other" flavors of ice cream besides chocolate, vanilla, and strawberry. Do another survey in your class to see which of those flavors are the class favorites!

_____

_____

_____

_____

OCEAN MAMMALS

Objective(s):

Students will...

• analyze and record on a chart numerical and statistical data about ocean mammals.

Materials Needed:

• computer
• student activity sheet

Web Site(s):

• http://www.seaworld.org/animal_bytes/walrusab.html
• http://www.seaworld.org/animal_bytes/bluewhaleab.html
• http://www.seaworld.org/animal_bytes/dolphinab.html

Teaching the Lesson:

This activity may take two class periods. Students can work in groups of two or three, depending on their level. As with any lesson that emphasizes statistical data, creates charts and graphs, etc., be sure to indicate the importance of recording information in an organized form for future reference.

NCTM Standards: 1, 2, 3, 4, 6, 9, 10, 11, 13

OCEAN MAMMALS

Name: _____

Date: _____

Go to:

http://www.seaworld.org/animal_bytes/walrusab.html

Read on this page the information about the walrus. Then answer the following questions.

1. How many walruses are living in the world today?

   _____

2. How many pounds do male walruses weigh?

   _____

3. About how many inches thick is the walrus blubber?

   _____

4. How big are adult walruses?

   _____

Go to:

http://www.seaworld.org/animal_bytes/bluewhaleab.html

Read the information about the blue whale.

5. About how many blue whales are living today?

   _____

6. How many pounds do blue whales weigh?

   _____

7. How many blue whales usually travel together?

   _____

8. How big are blue whales?

   _____

OCEAN MAMMALS *(cont.)*

Name: _____

Date: _____

Go to:

http://www.seaworld.org/animal_bytes/dolphinab.html

Read the information about the bottlenose dolphin.

9. How much do adult bottlenose dolphins weigh?

_____

10. How big are adult bottlenose dolphins?

_____

11. How many dolphins usually travel together in a pod (group)?

_____

Making a Chart

Doctor Crow, your friend the scientist at Marine World, wants you to do her a favor. She is studying the differences among walruses, blue whales, and bottlenose dolphins. Doctor Crow knows that you have learned some things about these animals on the Internet, and she would like you to make a chart of this information.

Fill out the chart below, using the information you have written down on the previous pages.

Animal	Size	Weight	Number of Tusks
Walrus			
Blue Whale			
Bottlenose Dolphin			

CHILLY TODAY, COLD TAMALE

Objective(s):

Students will...

- find out current weather-related information as they interact with the Web sites.
- compare weather patterns in different regions of the U.S.

Materials Needed:

- student activity sheet
- computer

Web Site(s):

- http://www.weather.com/twc/homepage.twc
- http://www.weatherpost.com/longterm/historical/data/honolulu_hawaii.htm
- http://www.weatherpost.com/wp-srv/weather/longterm/historical/data/buffalo_ny.htm
- http://www.city.net/countries/united_states/new_york/buffalo
- http://www.city.net/countries/united_states/hawaii/honolulu

Teaching the Lesson:

Explain to students how weather information is gathered and that this information is fed into a database that they will access. Emphasize careful navigation through the site and monitor progress carefully. This is a good geography or weather science-related springboard.

NCTM Standards: 1, 2, 3, 4, 6, 8, 11, 13

CHILLY TODAY, COLD TAMALE

Name: _____

Date: _____

Go to:

http://www.weather.com/twc/homepage.twc

Click on the link that says "US City Forecasts."

Our first city that we will visit is Seattle, Washington. Type the word Seattle where it says "Enter a city." Then click on the "go city" button.

1. What is the temperature right now in Seattle?

   _____

2. What kind of weather is expected for tomorrow?

   _____

3. Is the temperature over the next five days going to go up, go down, or both?

   _____

Click the "back" button on your browser.

Enter a new city in the space where you had Seattle typed. Now type in "Cincinnati."

4. What is the temperature right now in Cincinnati?

   _____

5. What kind of weather is expected tomorrow?

   _____

6. Will the temperarture go up, go down, or stay the same over the next five days?

   _____

7. What is the difference in temperature between Seattle and Cincinnati today?

   _____

CHILLY TODAY, COLD TAMALE *(cont.)*

Name: _____

Date: _____

Let's compare the weather over a long period of time in two very different cities. The information on these Web pages has been gathered for the last 24 years, and some of it for the last 40 years! Our first city will be Honolulu, Hawaii.

Go to:

http://www.weatherpost.com/longterm/historical/data/honolulu_hawaii.htm

1. Pick a winter, spring, and summer month. Write down the names of the months you picked.

   winter   spring   summer

   _____   _____   _____

Move down the Web page to where it says "Average Snowfall."

2. How much snowfall was there in each of these three seasons?

   _____   _____   _____

Move up the page to find "Lowest Recorded Temperature."

3. What is the lowest recorded temperature in each of the months that you chose?

   _____   _____   _____

Now we'll visit the Web page for a very different city—Buffalo, New York.

Go to:

http://www.weatherpost.com/wp-srv/weather/longterm/historical/data/buffalo_ny.htm

Remember the months that you chose for each season? Let's find the information for each of those months for Buffalo, New York.

CHILLY TODAY, COLD TAMALE *(cont.)*

Name: _____

Date: _____

4. How many inches of snow fell in each of the three months that you chose?

   _____   _____   _____

5. What was the lowest recorded temperature in each of those months?

   _____   _____   _____

Now we can compare these two very different parts of the United States.

6. How much more snow fell in Buffalo compared with Honolulu in each of the three seasons you have studied?

   _____

7. How much colder was it in Buffalo compared with Honolulu in each of the three months you studied?

   _____   _____   _____

Let's pretend that you are grown up and have been offered a great job in Buffalo and a great job in Honolulu. Where would you want to live and work? Explain why you feel this way.

_____

_____

_____

_____

SCAVENGER HUNT

Objective(s):

Students will...

- locate numerical information from various Web sites and record it.

Materials Needed:

- student activity sheet
- computer

Web Site(s):

- http://www.f50.com/contents.cfm
- http://www.box.net.au/~ciaran/Towers.html
- http://www.gorp.com/gorp/resource/US_National_Forest/ca/see_iny1.htm
- http://www.niagaraconservation.com/ultimate.htm
- http://www.wvi.com/~lelandh/sr-71~1.htm
- http://elo.www.media.mit.edu/people/elo/cia/Nauru.html
- http://www.netway.com/~carlton/tuna.htm
- http://popularmechanics.com/popmech/sci/tech/9512TUTRWM.html
- http://www.dialspace.dial.pipex.com/agarman/cheetah.htm

Teaching the Lesson:

This lesson will be of interest to all students as they explore the Internet, looking for interesting numerical information. It is more structured than some other "scavenger hunts" to make it appropriate for a variety of levels. This is a good starting point for any activities related to the topics on these pages.

NCTM Standards: 4, 11, 13

SCAVENGER HUNT

Name: _____

Date: _____

You and your partner are going to be a part of an Internet scavenger hunt. Just like any other kind of scavenger hunt, you will be "collecting" things. As Internet scavengers, you will collect information! As you visit different Web sites, you will be asked to answer questions and write down facts about the places you go.

Go to:

http://www.f50.com/contents.cfm

1. Find out how fast a Ferrari F50 can go!

_____

Go to:

http://www.box.net.au/~ciaran/Towers.html

2. How tall is the world's tallest building?

_____

Go to:

http://www.gorp.com/gorp/resource/US_National_Forest/ca/see_iny1.htm

3. How old is the oldest tree in the world?

_____

Go to:

http://dialspace.dial.pipex.com/agarman/cheetah.htm

4. How fast can a cheetah run?

_____

Go to:

http://www.niagaraconservation.com/ultimate.htm

5. How much water goes down the drain when you flush the toilet?

_____

SCAVENGER HUNT *(cont.)*

Name: _____

Date: _____

Go to:

http://www.wvi.com/~lelandh/sr-71~1.htm

6. What is the name of the world's fastest airplane?

_____

Go to:

http://elo.www.media.mit.edu/people/elo/cia/Nauru.html

7. What is the world's smallest country?

_____

Go to:

http://www.netway.com/~carlton/tuna.htm

8. How many pounds can a bluefin tuna weigh?

_____

Go to:

http://popularmechanics.com/popmech/sci/tech/9512TUTRWM.html

9. What is the fastest train in the world?

_____

DRIVE THAT CAR

Objective(s):

Students will...

- determine fractions of a car by examining its parts.

Materials Needed:

- computer
- student activity sheet

Web Site(s):

- http://www.caranddriver.com

Teaching the Lesson:

This simple lesson allows students to practice their fraction skills and link the fractions with tangible objects. By bringing in your own model cars or other objects with similarly proportioned parts, this lesson can be extended significantly.

NCTM Standards: 1, 2, 3, 4, 6, 12, 13

DRIVE THAT CAR!

Name: _____

Date: _____

Go to:

http://www.caranddriver.com

Look at a car on this Web page. Answer the questions below.

1. How many tires does the car have?

   _____

2. How many doors do you see?

   _____

3. Let's say the car drove over a very rough road. One of the tires got a flat.
   You could say that ____ out of ____ tires is flat. Another way of saying this is
   as a fraction, ____/____.

4. You went shopping in this car for new tire. While you were waiting, a
   shopping cart slammed into the driver's door. ____ out of ____ doors is now
   damaged. What fraction of the doors is damaged? ____/____.

ALL ABOARD!

Objective(s):

Students will...

- access travel information on the Internet.
- create an itinerary for travel from a particular destination to another.

Materials Needed:

- computer
- student activity sheet

Web Site(s):

- http://www.quickaid.com/~qrail/routing/
- http://www.quickaid.com/~qrail/routing/routes.cgi?origin=SAN&destination=EKA
- http://www.sandiego.org/
- http://city.net/countries/united_states/california/eureka/

Teaching the Lesson:

Students should become familiar with the process of train travel through this activity. It is an excellent starting point to discuss modern methods of transportation and the demise of public train transportation over the past 40 years. Further, students will have the chance to explore the two major cities in this activity, so some history can be integrated into this lesson as well.

NCTM Standards: 1, 2, 3, 4, 6, 7, 8, 10, 13

ALL ABOARD

Name: _____

Date: _____

Go to:

http://www.quickaid.com/~qrail/routing/

It's time to take a vacation again! You are going to travel along the beautiful California coastline aboard a train.

Your starting point will be San Diego in southern California, and your destination is Eureka in the northern part of the state.

Directions:

Qrail will figure out the fastest way for you to travel by train. If necessary, you will take a bus part of the way as well. Use the buttons to highlight where you are leaving from (San Diego) and where you will travel to (Eureka).

Then click the button at the bottom of the page or click where it says Route #1.

1. How long will the trip take?

   _____

2. How many trains will you take?

   _____

3. Will you be taking a bus? How many of them?

   _____

4. What time will you be leaving from San Diego?

   _____

5. What time will you arrive in Eureka?

   _____

ALL ABOARD *(cont.)*

Name: _____

Date: _____

Click where it says Route #1.

6. Where will your first bus take you?

   _____

7. How many cities will you stop in along the way?

   _____

8. List the cities you will stop at on the way from San Diego to Eureka.

   _____

Your next assignment is to find out about some of the places you will stop at on this trip.

Go to:

http://www.sandiego.org/

Click on one of the links that seems interesting. Write down three interesting facts about San Diego.

_____

_____

_____

Go to:

http://city.net/countries/united_states/california/eureka/

Click on a subject about this area that interests you.

Write down three interesting facts about Eureka as well.

_____

_____

_____

BACKYARD LEMONADE

Objective(s):

Students will...

- calculate fractions.
- examine proportions.
- determine how to divide up profits from a business.

Materials Needed:

- computer
- student activity sheet

Web Site(s):

- http://www.sunkist.com

Teaching the Lesson:

In this lesson, the example given is well-known to students: the lemonade stand. This presents a chance for real-life activities, depending on your wish for connections by the students. You can extend this activity by bringing in lemons, making lemonade, and determining the fractions of the various ingredients. Also a link to money can be made if you wish to discuss selling the lemonade.

BACKYARD LEMONADE

Name: _____

Date: _____

Go to:

http://www.sunkist.com

Look at the pictures of fresh lemons.

Directions: Read and carefully answer the questions below.

Sergio has a friend named Ernesto. In Ernesto's backyard, there is a beautiful young lemon tree. The lemon tree has 45 lemons growing on it.

Ernesto wanted to make lemonade, so he brought 15 lemons over to Sergio.

1. Write down a fraction that shows how many lemons were taken from the lemon tree.

   _____

2. Sergio inspected the lemons. He saw that three of them were not yet ripe. What fraction of the lemons Ernesto picked were NOT ripe?

   _____

3. How many ripe lemons were left over for lemonade?

   _____

4. After Sergio and Ernesto squeezed the lemons, they had two cups of lemon juice. To make lemonade, they needed to add four times the amount of water as juice. How many cups of water would they use to make the lemonade?

   _____

5. Look at the question above. How many cups of lemonade did Sergio and Ernesto end up making?

   _____

6. Suppose the two boys agreed to sell each cup of lemonade for 25 cents. If they sold eight cups of lemonade, how much money did they make?

   _____

TRUCK AND TRAILER FRACTIONS

Objective(s):

Students will...

- determine the fractions of a truck needed to make up a whole truck.

Materials Needed:

- computer
- student activity sheet

Web Site(s):

- http://www.mayflowertransit.com

Teaching the Lesson:

This activity is ideally part of a fractions-based lesson where students can think of the entire truck as the "whole" divided into various sections based on the number of wheels asked for in the questions. Discussing the reasons why trucks this size need 18 or more wheels is an opportunity for a follow-up to this lesson.

NCTM Standards: 1, 2, 3, 4, 6, 12, 13

TRUCK AND TRAILER FRACTIONS

Name: _____

Date: _____

Go to:

http://www.mayflowertransit.com

Directions: Answer the questions below about what you see on this Web page.

1. Look carefully at this vehicle. How many wheels does it have with the trailer attached?

    _____

2. How many wheels would there be with two trailers attached?

    _____

3. If the truck drove away without the trailer (also known as a bobtail) ____ out

    of _____ wheels would be left behind. A fraction that means the same thing

    is ____/_____.

WHEN IN ROME

Objective(s):

Students will...

- identify and apply the Roman numeral system to solve computational problems.

Materials Needed:

- computer
- student activity sheet

Web Site(s):

- http://www.salesonline.com/ijams/roman02.htm
- http://www.salesonline.com/ijams/roman01.htm

Teaching the Lesson:

This lesson can be linked with the lessons on the Mayan number system. Show students examples (such as copyrights on a television show) that are often written in Roman numerals. Discuss the limitations and advantages of this system.

NCTM Standards: 1, 2, 3, 4, 6, 7, 8, 9, 13

WHEN IN ROME (cont.)

Name: _____

Date: _____

You already know that the ancient Romans had a different counting system from the one we use today. For instance, instead of writing "10," an ancient Roman would write "X." Sometimes, we still use Roman numerals. Did you know the name of every Superbowl is always written in Roman numerals?

Go to:

http://www.salesonline.com/ijams/roman02.htm

Write down the Roman numerals for the following numbers:

1 _____

5 _____

10 _____

20 _____

25 _____

50 _____

75 _____

100 _____

Roman numerals can be cumbersome to write. The year 1998 is written MCMXCVIII.

Wow! No wonder we switched to a different system. Now, let's add together some Roman numerals. Be sure to write your answer as a Roman numeral too.

Go to:

http://www.salesonline.com/ijams/roman01.htm to help you.

1. I + I = _____

2. II + II = _____

3. V + V = _____

4. X + X = _____

5. XV + XV = _____

MAYAN MATH

Objective(s):

Students will...

- learn simple Mayan numbers and compute with them.

Materials Needed:

- computer
- student activity sheet

Web Site(s):

- http://www.baxter.net/edunet/cat/timemachine/mayanum.html

Teaching the Lesson:

Teaching other number systems is an excellent multicultural math experience. This is a good time to begin teaching students about Mayan history and to discuss what the limitations of these early mathematical systems were. Some students will need individual help to make the initial connection between the symbols and our number system.

NCTM Standards: 1, 2, 3, 4, 5, 6, 7, 9, 13

MAYAN NUMBERS

Name: _____

Date: _____

One thousand five hundred years ago, the Mayan people had their own number system. Here's your chance to learn about it!

Go to:

http://www.baxter.net/edunet/cat/timemachine/mayanum.html

You can see from the list of numbers that Mayans used dots and bars for their numbers. One dot means one, two dots mean the number two, and so on.

1. Write the Mayan numbers for

   Three

   Four   _____

   The other Mayan number symbol, the bar, means five. One bar means five, two bars mean ten, and so on. Being able to count by fives is very helpful in Mayan math!

2. Write the Mayan numbers for

   fifteen: _____

   twenty: _____

   The Mayans, like the Romans, added these symbols together to make numbers too. For instance, the number seven would be

   $$\bullet \ \bullet$$
   $$\rule{2cm}{1mm}$$

   which is the same as 5 + 2 = 7.

3. Write down the Mayan numbers (be sure the dots are above the bars, as in the examples) for

   six: _____

   thirteen: _____

MAYAN MATH

Name: _____

Date: _____

Go to:

http://www.baxter.net/edunet/cat/timemachine/mayanum.html

One other symbol besides the • and the — was used in Mayan numbers. That was the symbol for zero. Look on the Web page and find the Mayan symbol for zero. Then draw it on the back.

Write out the following math problems, using Mayan symbols.

1. six plus four equals ten

2. two plus one equals three

3. nine minus nine equals zero

4. one minus zero equals one

5. eighteen minus six equals twelve

SECRET CODES AND MESSAGES

Objective(s):

Students will...

- become familiar with the Morse code and apply it to uncover a secret message.

Materials Needed:

- computer
- student activity sheet

Web Site(s):

- http://www.soton.ac.uk/~scp93ch/refer/alphabet.html#punctuation

Teaching the Lesson:

This lesson should be done in pairs. Discuss with students why a code was important during wartime and why Morse was used in the past when no voice communication was possible. You may want to go around and check that students have written down the correct code for each letter. One misplaced dot or dash could change everything!

The answer for the decoded message on the third work sheet of this activity is "Math is the most important subject you will ever learn."

NCTM Standards: 1, 2, 3, 4, 6, 9, 13

SECRET CODES AND MESSAGES

Name: _____

Date: _____

Morse code is an easy way to "spell" words without using letters. Just by making sounds, you can spell words. Morse code is made of just two sounds. A dash (-) is a long beep. That's the same as the - in Morse code. The other sound in Morse code is a dot. The dot sounds like a short beep.

Beep BEEEEP can be written .- (dot dash). You have just seen the Morse code for the letter A!

Now you can see all the letters in the English language in Morse code.

Go to:

http://www.soton.ac.uk/~scp93ch/refer/alphabet.html#punctuation

Write the code for each letter. BE CAREFUL! Only write the code for English letters. That is the first one in each group.

Letter	Code	Letter	Code	Letter	Code
A	_____	J	_____	S	_____
B	_____	K	_____	T	_____
C	_____	L	_____	U	_____
D	_____	M	_____	V	_____
E	_____	N	_____	W	_____
F	_____	O	_____	X	_____
G	_____	P	_____	Y	_____
H	_____	Q	_____	Z	_____
I	_____	R	_____		

SECRET CODES AND
MESSAGES *(cont.)*

Name: _____

Date: _____

Using the information you wrote on the previous page, write down the Morse code for the words below. Important information: After each code letter, write a "/" to separate them so you don't get mixed up.

Look at the first example below.

Word	Code
CAT	-.-./.-/-
DOG	_____
FISH	_____
BOX	_____
Your Name	_____

134

SECRET CODES AND MESSAGES *(cont.)*

Name: _____

Date: _____

Decode the secret message that is written in Morse code below.

--/ .-/ -/ ..../   ../ .../   -/ ..../ ./

| | | | | | | | | | | |

--/ ---/ .../ -/   ../ --/ .--./ ---/ .-./ -/ .-/ -./ -/

| | | | | | | | | | | | | | |

.../ ..-/ -.../ .---/ ./ -.-./ -/   -.--/ ---/ ..-/

| | | | | | | | | | | |

.--/ ../ .-../ .-../   ./ ...-/ ./ .-./   .-../ ./ .-/ .-./ -./

| | | | | | | | | | | | | | | |

BICYCLE BUILT FOR WHOM?

Objective(s):

Students will...

- determine the correct combination of bicycle parts needed for various numbers of bicycles to be constructed.

Materials Needed:

- computer
- student activity sheet

Web Site(s):

- http://www.crupiparts.com/ or
- http://library.advanced.org/10333/mtn_bikers/get_start/what_mtn/index.html

Teaching the Lesson:

These word problems can also be drawn on the board as a math equation. This will help students to see that using equations can help thems solve word problems. Making additional examples of these questions would be an excellent supplement to this lesson. You can even use parts to put together a model using Lego-type materials.

NCTM Standards: 1, 2, 3, 4, 6, 7, 8, 13

BICYCLE BUILT FOR WHOM?

Name: _____

Date: _____

Go to:

http://www.crupiparts.com/

http://library.advanced.org/10333/mtn_bikers/get_start/what_mtn/index.html

Learn out about bicycles and answer the questions below.

1. Suppose you are a custom bike builder. You build bikes for professional mountain-bike riders. Your team of six riders is depending on you to build one main bike and one spare for each team member in time for the next race. Now it is time to order parts to build the bikes. How many wheels will you need?

   _____

2. How many frames will you need?

   _____

3. One of the bikes was badly damaged in a pre-race practice run. The only part of the bike that can be reused is the frame. Name six other parts that you will need to make this bike race ready.

   _____

   _____

   _____

   _____

   _____

PLAY BALL!

Objective(s):

Students will...

- determine the "movement" of a football through a series of word problems.

Materials Needed:

- student activity sheet
- computer

Web Site(s):

- http://www.utexas.edu/athletics/tickets/football/stadium.html

Teaching the Lesson:

This lesson does not depend on any prior knowledge about the game of football, but a short primer might help some students. Monitor lower-level students' progress through the problems. Grouping them together might be an option here.

NCTM Standards: 1, 2, 3, 4, 6, 7, 10

PLAY BALL!

Name: _____

Date: _____

Go to:

http://www.utexas.edu/athletics/tickets/football/stadium.html

A football field is 100 yards long. There are 10 yards between each line on the field.

Look carefully at the drawing of the football field on this page. Each side of the field is 50 yards long. In the middle of the field is the 50-yard line. To get a touchdown, a player has to take the ball past the 50-yard line toward the other team's 40, 30, 20, and 10-yard line and finally score a touchdown.

1. How many lines must you cross to get from one end of the field to the other?

   _____

2. How many yards must a player travel to get from the 20-yard line to the 50-yard line?

   _____

3. Suppose a player catches the ball at the 10-yard line after a kickoff. How far must he run to get to the 50-yard line?

   _____

Two teams are playing on the football field, the Warhawks and the Jackals. The Jackals will kick off.

4. The kickoff is caught by the Warhawks at their 20-yard line! The Warhawks player runs hard and is tackled at his own 40-yard line. How far did the player run with the ball?

   _____

5. The Warhawks hike the ball, and the quarterback passes the ball 20 yards! The Warhawks receiver is immediately tackled. What yard line are the Warhawks on now?

   _____

A TURN FOR THE WORDS

Objective(s):

Students will...

- define and apply math prefixes to words.

Materials Needed:

- computer
- student activity sheet

Web Site(s):

- http://www.infoseek.com/Facts?pg=deskref.html

Teaching the Lesson:

This can be part of your language arts lessons or independent work time. There are many other math-related prefixes and suffixes that students can work on after doing this activity.

NCTM Standards: 2, 3, 4, 6, 13

A TURN FOR THE WORDS

Name: _____

Date: _____

Prefixes are at the beginning of a word, and some mean a certain number. For instance, you know that a bicycle has two wheels. The prefix "bi" at the beginning of the word tells you that. A tricycle has _____ wheels.

See if you can think of some words with number prefixes in them. Here is a list of prefixes to help you get started.

Uni- means one of something.	Mono- also means one of something.
Bi- means two of something.	Di- also means two of something.
Tri- means three of something.	
Quad- means four of something.	
Penta- means five of something.	Quint- also means five of something.

Say each of these prefixes out loud one at a time. Then write some words that use these prefixes.

_____

_____

_____

_____

_____

Use the Internet dictionary to find more words with numbers in them.

Go to:

http://www.infoseek.com/Facts?pg=deskref.html

Type in a word to check the meanings of the words.

DEFINITELY MATH

Objective(s):

Students will...

- define important math terms and apply them to sentences.

Materials Needed:

- Computer
- Student activity sheet

Web Site(s):

- http://www.astro.virginia.edu/~eww6n/math/math.html

Teaching the Lesson:

Some of the words in this group will be challenging to certain students. Give them extra help with pronunciation as needed. Take any of the words in this lesson as a starting point for a lesson on that topic!

NCTM Standards: 2, 3, 4, 6, 7, 13

DEFINITELY MATH

Name: _____

Date: _____

Go to:

http://www.astro.virginia.edu/~eww6n/math/math.html

Find the words on the list below. Write down what they mean.

abacus _____

bisect _____

concave _____

digit _____

equilateral triangle _____

geometry _____

hectare _____

hexagon _____

knot _____

Go to the next page for more instructions and a chance to use these vocabulary words.

DEFINITELY MATH *(cont.)*

Name: _____

Date: _____

Using the definitions of the words on the previous page, fill in the correct word in each sentence.

1. Long before people invented calculators, the Chinese used the _____ to help them add up large numbers.

2. Each of the numbers 1, 2, 3, 4, and 5 are also known as _____.

3. To make sure her shoe didn't fall off while playing, Gina tied a double _____.

4. Donny's parents bought a house in the country with one _____ of land around it.

5. The stop sign was shaped like a _____.

6. If you want to learn anything about shapes, you must learn some _____.

7. "Let's _____ the last cookie," said Rudy. "That way you and I will each get half."

8. "All three of us need to stand an equal distance away from each other while we play catch," said Jasper, "just like an _____ _____."

9. A runaway shopping cart made a _____ dent in Marianne's car door.